Gospel Desert

NEHEMY N. KIHARA

DEDICATION

Dedicated to all the children of Pastoral Nomads in Northern Kenya, African Sahara Desert Region and in the Global Arid Regions.

Dedicated to my late beloved brother Philip Wahome Kihara, who served his country as a warrior in the General Service Unit(GSU),the Anti-Stock Theft Unit (ASTU) and the Airport Police Unit (APU).

He endured many hardships in the deserts and forests surrounding Northern Kenya as a Police Officer ,securing peace and serving all.

Dedicated also to the children he left us, who sincerely call me dad-Clinton Kihara, Derik Masero ,Evaras Wanjiru,Movin Njoki ,and their dear mother-Leah Apondi Masero Wahome..

The book is also a dedication to all other children who call me father-Evaras Wanjiru Kihara, Zipora Wanjiku Kihara-Hearly,

Isabel Wairimu(Njoki)Kihara,

Mutava(Kihara)Ndirangu, sister Mbinyu Ndirangu,

Wanjiru(Ciru) and brother Joseph Ndirangu Kaiga and their beloved mothers.

Lastly but not least I dedicate the book to all my grandchildren

Ezraella Wanjiru(Ciru) Clark, Nathaniel Ndirangu James; Nia(Ciru)

Ndirangu James, Madison Wanjiru(Ciru)Hearly,

Jameson Alex Ndirangu Hearly

and Jade (Ciru) Wahington

and all others that the Lord grants us.

CONTENTS

ACKNOWLEDGMENTS

Many thanks go to my research and history of religion lecturer at
St. Paul's University (United Theological College)- Rev. William
Anderson, American missionary to Sudan and East Africa.
My first research tour colleague-Dieter Lorenz of
Hamburg University, Germany.
My second research tour companion and Kenyan-American
Educator Mwalimu Dr. Esther Wanjiru-Kihara, granddaughter of the
great Senior Chief Karanja Kibarabara of Murang'a County.
My Sikh cousins Santock Singh and Gurnam Singh; for
hosting us at Mandera
Rev. Dr. Plawson Kuria, former Secretary General of the
Presbyterian Church of East Africa hosting us at
Maralal,,where he was Parish Priest
the Catholic Church Italian Missionaries in Marsabit, Wajir and
Garissa who graciously hosted us and shared
great firsthand information.
To the many Kenyan Police and Army security officers
who assisted me.
I am grateful. to all of you.

1 INTRODUCTION

A.   Definition of the Subject

1.What is Evangelism?

One of the questions of this research is the "Problem of Evangelism in the predominantly Muslim Northern Kenya, as the Yet Evangelized."

Evangelism unfortunately, has been misunderstood many times, especially in our country and all over the world. It has suffered more than any other word in the whole Christian vocabulary.

It is interesting to hear such words as mercenary, superficial, unethical, mystical, professional, extra, occasional emotional, offensive, high pressure and unnecessary being used to describe and qualify it.

This, however, has only confused many people of what Evangelism really is. Evangelism, means, the presentation of the message of redemption or liberation by the Savior-Lord Jesus Christ.

It is the presentation of the Evangel, the God-Spell, or the Good News.

Evangelism, therefore, deals with people, their situations and problems. In other words, it is a social therapy. This is a fact revealed and supported by history; that is, where Evangelism is taken seriously, it has dealt with social problems in a progressive way. Caring for people and their need for food, shelter, education, health, and, above all, a new outlook on life.

Evangelism, therefore, becomes a service for the wholeness of man, carrying in its nature the compassion of Jesus Christ--the only balancer of both the social and spiritual need of man, for He became once God in man; that is the Divine incarnated into humanity.

Evangelism should be the uplifting and showing forth of the Liberator--Jesus Christ, so that men may see Him and by seeing Him may believe in Him whose coming to this world has completely transformed the human situation and made available a totally new life and culture to all mankind.

2.Reason for Evangelism

Evangelism is of vital importance for the totality of the whole person. Every human being needs God in life; they need to experience deep inside , the love of the concerned Good Shepherd.

They need to meet the Son of the loving Father, who gives salvation and liberation of the whole person through His shed blood on the Cross of Calvary, giving peace and continual comfort by the Holy Spirit.

For this reason, the Church must evangelize, not only for the spiritual Dimension in mankind, but also for a social change expressing the deep love and compassion for the souls of people lost without response to god as revealed in the person of His Soon--God Jesus Christ.

Evangelism is also essential for the edification of the Body of Christ, for by evangelizing we bring to a confused world the realization that the only panacea for a world in chaos is Jesus Christ whose administrative presence alone in the Holy Spirit can resolve the world's state of hopelessness.

The Church must be committed to the constant duty of leading people to the knowledge of the Lord by bringing them to a point of conversion or new birth (John 3:3).

2 RESEARCH SCOPE:: ECOLOGY AND

GEOGRAPHY

B. The Scope of the Research

1. Places Visited

The purpose of this research and book is to crystalize and present in written form the problem that affects the Church's mission in Northern Kenya (East Africa) which has been closed to missionary work for more than half a century.

The report and challenges contained here is a result of many weeks of investigation (and more than three years of observation) in the sweeping deserts of the former Northern Kenya District (NFD), as named by the British Colonial Administration

.

Before devolution to county governance it was administered under three provinces namely, Rift Valley, Eastern and North Eastern.

The research is limited in its scope, partly because of time and means of travel. The writer, however, travelled extensively in all the districts in Northern Kenya, apart from one--Turkana.

Through observation and casual conversation from the people that the writer met, ranging from local people, up-country Christians and government administrators, he came to understand the situation in Northern Kenya more clearly than he had ever understood before.

This research began in 1970 when the writer was a ministerial student at St. Paul's United Theological College, Limuru, which had made it possible to make a trip to this area, accompanied by Dieter Lorenz of Hamburg University, Germany.

The first step started from Isiolo, then westward to Maralal in Samburu County and to Baragoi. and South Hor

Unable to go across to Turkana County, the writer had to return to Isiolo County and proceed further north in Marsabit County to Moyale, then south of Ethiopia and back to Moyale through Buna to Wajir County and Garissa County, returning back to Wajir.

It was impossible at this period to proceed to Mandera (which was reached in the second trip in 1974, accompanied by school teacher wife Esther Wanjiru Kihara, a grand-daughter of the Maasai-Gikuyu Loc.6 (Muthithi, Murang'a County late Senior Chief Karanja Kibarabara [Ol'Nyagusie,-Maasai age group]

His father Sr Chief Kibarabara was supposed to have been a Tanzanian Maasai from the Coast of Kenya, Karanja Kibarabara was cousin of late Senior Chief Letoya Ole Kaparo of Doldol in Laikipia County, who confirmed this to the author during a culture festival..

The Author returned and put his findings into a short written form. This report was presented at Limuru Conference Center to a joint Germany and Kenyan Theological Students Project.

This book also contains the findings from the second trip which started from Murang'a County to Isiolo and Wajir, then to Mandera, visiting both Ethiopia again and Somalia Republic and coming back through Wajir, Garissa, and Thika.in Kiambu County

The reason for wanting to visit all of the present seven counties in Northern Kenya is to have a general view and observation of the local situation. But, unfortunately, the far northwest Turkana County was impassible.

In the second trip, the writer was able, after almost five years, to visit Mandera County (far northeastern). Turkana County and its local situation, however, is similar to the surrounding places which the writer was able to visit in spite of the problem of transportation which will be discussed later.

2. **People Observed**

The main groups in these places are mostly nomadic people who graze their cattle, goats, camels and donkeys on an ever shifting pastureland.

Turkana(Estimated to be 1.1 million in 2016, which was 1.8% of Kenyan population of 47.1 m.)

On the far northwest lies the Turkana land which strictly occupies about 23,457 square miles. It is below the escarpment on the Rift Valley floor where there is a dramatic change in vegetation.

Here cattle are found in scattered areas, especially on mountains or by riverbanks, unless there has been exceptionally good rains. The county is adequate in most parts for goats, sheep, camels, and donkeys are found everywhere.

Turkana land is said to suffer from poorer climate and only the camel is able to survive. Even near Lake (Rudolf) Turkana and Central Turkana, the land becomes sheer desert.

Samburu(Estimated in 2016, to be 0.50% of Kenyan population)

The next neighborhood to Turkana land is Samburu land. The Samburu are mostly a northerly Maa-speakers.(they are cousins of the Maasai community, which is estimated to be about 1 million in Kenya and 1.3 m. total; in additional of those in Tanzania.)

Moreover, because of inter-marriage with the Turkana, a lot of Turkana can be found in this impenetrable land, due to rock and lava between the uplands and the Lake (Rudolf) Turkana which is essentially in Samburu County. ,due to rock and lava desert..

Redille (0.17% of Kenyan population)

Above the Samburu are the Redille who are Cushite language speakers and live mostly in Marsabit. It is interesting that their language bears some resemblance to Somali. But their dress and customs are different and have, in fact, more in common with those of the Samburu and Maasai. Someone said that they form a wedge between `traditional-Afro-theist' and Muslim Borana/Oromo.

Coming into the actual N.F.D. which the author mentioned while speaking about the Redille of Marsabit, we find the Moyale sub-county next to Marsabit which adjoins Samburu.

Here we come upon the Islamized Borana in the eastern part while on the Western part, we find the so called `traditionalist' who hold traditional or indigenous beliefs as others about God). Oromo-Borana, Gabbra, Sakuye and Orma..

The Borana are classified as Cushite, they are part of the Oromo [formerly called Galla] people--namely, the Gabbra, (Estimated in 2016, to be 0.15% of Kenyan population of 47.1m) Sakuye, (Estimated in 2016, to be 0.04% of Kenyan population) and Orma; (Estimated in 2016, to be 0.15% of Kenyan population) the latter sharing almost half of the Marsabit County with the Redille.

The Borana-Oromo(with 187,000 2016 ,estimated population in Kenya) go beyond the Kenyan border into the southern part of Ethiopia (where they are estimated to be 1.4m-in population, and are a significant number of the Oromo community.)

Somali(*2.7 million-population estimate in 2016, which made them 6th largest community in Kenya*)

Another main group in Northern Kenya is that of the Somali. The Somalis are linguistically classified as Cushitic, with almost two-thirds of them living in the Somali Republic. (In visiting the Republic, the author found that one third live in Kenya and Ethiopia and there are several divided into several clans).

Also, a considerable number of Somali live in Garissa and Isiolo. Their main centers are Mandera and Wajir In Isiolo, Somali live among Borana , Meru and Agikuyu.

The Somali, like other groups in Northern Kenya, are nomadic people who graze their cattle and goats on even shifting pasture lands.

It is interesting to note that these Somali nomads, while grazing their camels and goats, take no notice of the legal boundaries when they search for water and grass. They often wander afar into Kenya and Ethiopia.

Ecology

Northern Kenya is scarcely inhabited. The ethnic groups mentioned here are the major ones, there are others who are a minority. .

There is a vast land with no sign of life, apart from a few animals or birds. In contrast with other parts of Kenya, this land is mainly red desert soils and calcareous sandy warms. This is why it is sparsely populated.

The land is good in the springtime, as this is the season for plenty. Rains fall, causing fresh grass to spring to life. There is an abundance of milk and meat. It contrasts vividly with the grueling months of draught that precede it.

Humans and some animals, like the camel, usually stand up to the severest draught. usually, in most cases, a woman with a young infant has to decide who is worthy of living. She has to decide between herself and the young one during prolonged draught.

When these wandering people come to a pasture they have shifted from before, they often claim it and raid each other's cattle; then the trouble begins.

This is followed by attacks and reprisals that escalate into ethnic wars. For example, the Somali versus Borana, the Samburu versus Turkana. Finally, exhaustion or famine ends the battling and things return to normal. We will see more about the culture, work, way of life and also the religion--tradition and Islam--of the Northern Kenya people in the next section.

3 PASTORAL SOCIETY AND NOMADIC CULTURE

THE CULTURAL PROBLEMS

A.   The People

1. <u>Their Work</u>

Large areas of Northern Kenya are sparsely populated. That is, they are nearly empty of people. The deserts and dry forests cover much of the country, providing little opportunity for people to make a living.

However, nomadic pastoralists wander over this vast area seeking good pastures for their cattle. Most of these desert nomads live in small shifting and self-made tents.

Others have simple shelters made of wood and skin; these are, by chance, those who live in the bushlands. The cattle sometimes crop the pastures so close to the ground that the grass dies. Therefore, the pastoralists must find new pastures.

The Turkana, unlike the ones described as shifting pastoralists, do not wander from place to place. Instead, they live in permanent villages called Kraals. These consists of group huts surrounded by fences. In the center is another fenced area for the animals. Most of the huts surrounded by the fence are round.

The Samburu have kraals too, made by plastering mud and cow dung over a framework of branches. The roofs are usually thatched with grass or palm leaves.

2. Their Way of Life

Most of the people in Northern Kenya, especially in the rural areas and also in the semi-urbanized town centers, seem idle because they do not have much to do. Life in these areas is very simple.

Those who really live in the Northern Kenya style live under primitive and ancient social forms, frequently at war with their neighbors.

The author observed that the Somali, especially in Mandera County and Somali Republic, prefer their own way of life and living in their own common beliefs. Since the last "Shifta War" with Kenya Government; which was caused by the claim for greater Somali, which meant the North seceding from the Republic of Kenya, they have come to enjoy peace and prosperity of independent Kenya Republic .

This independence lifted them from the colonial status and gave them pride and purpose because of its democratic foundation and principles. It has a constitution and administration content with their way of life and common beliefs

Somali

The average Somali is conscious of his own kinsmen, whether they live in either interior Somalia Republic, in the Republic of Ethiopia, or in Kenya. He has a deep feeling of his unity and clan brotherhood. However, the different clans and sections sometime divide them from their fellow kinsfolk.

The average Somali seem conservative in his view of life. He does not like sudden change and will resist it, if it seems contrary to his Islamic views. This, in most cases, results in a suspicion of strangers.

On occasions when he gathers with friends, he shares different views on current affairs. Discussions on the politics and religious achievement in Somalia and Arabic or Islamic countries, the social business, and trade (especially in his own vicinity) may take the whole day.

Turkana

The average Turkana, (Nilotic) also different in some ways from the Somali, is an independent individual. The Turkana I had met seemed very suspicious of strangers and is frequently down in disposition. However, they were fond of singing and dancing.

They seem to regard the welfare of his relatives and children as his first duty., despite of being seen as people who get excited by raiding their neighbors. To raise his spear against another Turkana is a social evil, and he cannot do it without feeling guilty conscious deep in his heart.

On rare occasions when he gathers with his friends, according to popular biased belief he seems boisterous and noisy.

However, in general, the Turkana are very acquisitive; and have a well-developed sense of hospitality. Some years ago, the mainspring of Turkana life was raiding. It was natural for the young men to go on raids after becoming of adult age. All Turkana wished to slay an enemy so that they could be known by hero names.

The Turkana cooperate in both their primary and secondary neighborhoods. In the primary neighborhood cooperation, men of the homesteads meet in a more or less personal way at a special shade tree and talk while the women visit each other.

At the same time, girls water the cattle at one water hole, while the boys herd. If the stock is not to be dispersed, the boys and girls play together in the pastures.

In the second neighborhood cooperation, the homesteads generally share one watering point, although a primary neighborhood may have a small water hole of its own which is sufficient for drinking water needs.

The village neighborhood does not act as a whole. Some of its inhabitants may be present at major events, especially weddings and dances.

Samburu

The Samburu (Nilotic) have the same cultural traits as the Maasai. Their only real occupation is keeping cattle and fighting ,which they now are deprived of, by modernity.

Many Samburu, especially in Maralal, have taken up cultivation, just as some Turkana and other groups have done. Others are employed as herdsmen on farms, while a great number does not consider such labor worthwhile to a Samburu.

The object on which the lives of the Samburu are centered is the cattle. Their importance is not only material but spiritual too. The whole existence of the Samburu depends on the cattle. To do any kind of work other than tend cattle means you are worthless and, therefore, despised by other Samburu.

They believe that in the beginning God gave them all the cattle in the world; therefore, nobody else has the right to possess any. This belief is also shared by the most northerly Maasai and the Nandi (Kalenjin).

Cattle, however, provide the Samburu with food in the form of milk, blood and meat.

They also give them mental and spiritual satisfaction through their existence, though it would seem that there is less outward and ritual expression of the love of cattle than among other group who combine pastoralism and agriculture.

Grass, being the food of cattle, also has a high ritual value and is used as a sign of peace. In Samburu, rivers are few and the rainfall low. The bush country is useless for grazing, as most of the rivers run close together.

Borana

Other groups have several cultural similarities with the Turkana, Somali and Samburu. For instance, the Borana, who are Cushite and speak the same Cushitic group language as the Somali, share many cultural similarities with the Somali.

The Borana culture, fortunately or unfortunately, remains indigenous because the British Colonial Administrators did not touch it much.

A few Borana have changed, just as in all other groups, because of mixing with people of different groups and places in their own Northern Kenya homelands, but their indigenous culture is still maintained.

This might be why some tourists considered them highly acquisitive, suspicious of strangers, unable to mix freely with them. Others considered the Borana as warlike with a sense of insecurity, always defensive and offensive in their attitude towards other people.

One of the customs they have maintained for a long time but now have been abandoned is that of cutting off a testicles of someone from another group (like the Somali or Turkana) which they show to their potential bride as a sign of strength and bravery.

This custom is mentioned here because it shows why other neighboring groups become aggressive in their attitude towards the Borana. Mainly, much of Borana culture has been mixed with Islam.

Redille (Cushitic)

The Redille, who are Borana neighbors, speak a language similar to that of the Samburu with whom they easily intermarry.

There were many other minor groups (such as the Dorobo) which the author came across. The author feels that there are many books and journals devoted to ethnographic surveys; therefore, he does not have to elaborate or give in details all the facts of the people in Northern Kenya, but the few he has mentioned are just for the sake of understanding the subject under observation.

 The main concern in to present the problems, as seen and experienced by the author, through a combination of direct observation and memory as he wrote his findings.

The author hopes this will challenge all concerned to act by keeping the exercise of giving the evangel of Jesus Christ, a more development approach, which means that the Church must evangelize by meeting the needs of whole person. (Matt. 28).

Education

To focus on one of the problems that come up from these different cultures, let us look at education. The people have just started seeing the value of education.

Mostly among the pastoralists, it is very hard to get the young boys to school because they have to look after cattle. It is even harder to get the girls to school, especially among the Islamized Borana and Somali who think that by sending the girls to school they will be exposed to the opposite sex and will, as a result, become prostitutes and forget their moral heritage.

The lack of education is widespread in Northern Kenya. The schools are few and the attendance is low compared with the local population. This makes them use different methods of resistance towards sending their children to school.

As a result, one of the most acute problems is created--the problem of ignorance or `backwardness.' Most people in Northern Kenya have started seeing what education can do and has done.

They keep resisting it despite the enlightenment it can bring to their own cultural values, way of behavior, and caring for their health. It is this lack of education that makes these people ignorant, poor and unprogressive in life.

Initiation

In almost all the groups, except the Turkana, initiations or circumcision of the boys and girls as soon as they reach puberty age is practiced. This practice makes the youth feel that he or she is now an adult and had learned all there is to learn in life. The girls then look forward to marriage, while the boys look forward to owning a herd of his own and settling down as head of family in his pastoral business or career.

Family Life

Family life among most of the groups suffers from many problems. Despite of the strong morality code against adultery, there are serious problems which come along, such as divorce or separation of the wife and husband.

This is true especially among the Islamized where there is a religious permission for a man to put his wife away for a while or even forever. He may withdraw his responsibility completely provided there is one witness. He then is free to have another wife, leaving the former wife to care for her problems forever.

This is against human principles because while the man enjoys the new relationship, his former wife starves. It is a fact that in an area like this, a mother is unable to push on life without a man's guidance as a husband.

The children start going wild as a result. The man never feels conscious of his evil actions because it is a part of his Muslim or Islamic convictions.

Population Growth

The population growth in northern Kenya is very low, compared with the other parts of Kenya, such as the Central Province. One of the causes that keep it low is the fact that there are too many problems that make most people sexually less active.

Sometimes children die after birth because of lack of medical care. Another problem, based on cultural differences, is "negative ethnocentrism," that is, each seeking his identity and basing his pride on his group alone as the only tribe worthy of living. This reflects a lack of understanding as to what to do next or where to go next, apart from the clan or ethnic group.

Mostly, ethnic feelings come along where a group has to graze their cattle on the other people's areas or where a national government official, working amongst people of his own group and clan, tends to discriminate against members of other ethnic groups.

4 RELIGIOUS PRACTICES AND BELIEF SYSTEMS

B. Religion

1.Indigenous

In order to get a view of the Indigenous religion that most of the people have in Northern Kenya, the author will cite only those groups still clinging to their Indigenous religion. It is notable that, it is in Northern Kenya that Dr. Leakey, the world renowned anthropologist, found the remains of the oldest man, near Lake Turkana.

The Islamized people will be dealt with later, with ignorance, underdevelopment or `backwardness', especially in Northern Kenya.

The Akuj 'Upward One'of Turkana;

The Turkana of the West Northern Kenya are extremely religious people. They acknowledge one High God, "Akuj", linguistically related to "Above or Up" (Uju).

This "Above One" or "Up One" lives above the clouds and is, by nature, benevolent, although he can send or take away diseases, hunger and other problems from humans.

When people die, they are believed to have gone to "Akuj" who can, in circumstances, strike down a person who commits incest or contravenes particularly an important ritual.

"Akuj" has constantly been induced to aid people, and all initiated men offer community prayers led by the most senior men at most meat feasts and at ceremonies such as weddings. Small personal prayer groups are held if one member of a family is ill or thought to be bewitched.

The chief representative of "Akuj" is the "Imuron" (diviner), but all holders of this title are not of the same status. The man who gradually acquires reputation for being in close contact with the High God "Akuj", the Above God, the Up one, is endowed with certain priest-like qualities.

He is distinguished or known as an "Imuron Akuj", the Above God-Diviner, or the Diviner of the Up One or the Diviner of the Above God.

The "Imuron Akuj" starts his career by a complete withdrawal from the society for a period which may vary from one or two nights to several months. Usually his means of subsistence and absence are surrounded by mystery as he takes stock with him and retires into an area that is usually deserted.

After the seclusion from society, "Imuron Akuj" returns, showing on his way inspiration with prophetic dreams and his success in predictions brings him a better chance of establishing enduring reputation.

"Imuron Akuj" foretells the future, combats witchcraft and sorcery, cures barrenness, purifies or fortifies age, heals the sick, sets and predicts successful raids and induces rain. This type of man was the most powerful in the past, providing the territorial districts or ethnic leaders who were greatly feared.

The Turkana, as a whole, are prosaic and, in general, uninfluenced by the magic of the religious side of life. When they can find a rational explanation, they will accept it and their beliefs do not enter into social relationships or economical activities.

The Enk-ai 'Great Sky One' of Samburu;

The Samburu, who were described before as Maa-Speakers like the Maasai (who share territory in both Kenya and Tanzania around Mt. Kilimanjaro), have little record of their religious beliefs except such obvious facts as the invocation of

"Enk-ai" (the word for God, rain and sky in Maasai, which is also shared by Bantu speakers such as Agikuyu, Embu, Meeru, and Akamba as 'Ngai-the Divider/Distributer, also rain in Ki-Meeru]

As of ancestor worship, it is generally said that the Maasai and Turkana do not believe in an afterlife.

However, to the Maasai and Samburu "Enkai", the One of the Sky, the one who gives rain, is recognized as a Creator and is prayed to, by all these people as the Only God.

But "Neiterkob", the mediator between God and humans, is seen as a minor deity; the word itself means "that Which begun the Earth" and thus would apply as a description of Enkai as Creator.

Enkai is grammatically feminine is male and his wife, "Ol-apa" Moon, is grammatically masculine. Which means there is female in the male, and the male in female. This gives us some confusion but does not necessarily lead us to disagree with the fact that God (Enkai) holds a supreme part in the Samburu life.

The Waqqa 'High One' of Borana;(Oromo)

The Borana are indigenous in their religion. Those who have been conquered by the Somali or those that are isolated are Islamized, a sign seen only in material objects such as ornaments and weapons.

The Borana have their own religion, and their personal and family rites are a mixture of Islamic concepts and practices although a higher God ("Waqqa") is acknowledged.

2.   **The Islamized**

Let us look at the Somali, almost 90 percent would say they are Muslims, despite of the fact that some define Islamic slightly different from other Sunni.

However, the idea of Islam as a way of life for the Somali has grown in the depth of their own lives, concepts and practices that it is very hard to see their tradition apart from Islam.. This has, however, caused a lot of problems, especially in the Northern Kenya.

In this area, the Somali and other Islamized minorities in other groups use the religion as a defensive mechanism against any change or development which would come along.

An example of this education which can do them a great deal of good. Instead, some still do not want western education. These rarely allow their girls to go to school because they fear that they will become prostitutes.

Their attitude towards modern development has proven to be dangerous because in the Northern Kenya, where Islam has its stronghold, idleness still is a major and main social ill.

People stay or sit near Mosques or Church/mission centers where available, talking for hours while their children, rugged and hungry, run all over the town.

The author's memory still recalls a lot of helpless children who jumped here and there looking for something to eat, especially in Wajir. However, God willing things are supposed to change, but even if it does not happen it is 'Shauri ya Mungu' that is, it is still in the 'Will of Allah'.

One would not be far from the truth to conclude that Islam, as a way of life in Northern Kenya, does give people a strong hope in God's gracious will to bless them.

Moreover, the Churches in some areas testify to the living God who loves people as his own children and, as their Father, blesses them with enjoyment of life abundantly.

Such an abundant life is a life that is not idle or based on fatalistic attitudes or behaviors that allow no change, growth or development. It is a life spent for the service of others, a life that is always concerned with the next neighbor and does something to help him as if he is a part of one's body. However, thanks to Almighty Omnipresent God, that in spite of this "idleness" and backwardness in development, all over Northern Kenya there is a sign of openness and hunger for the Gospel of the real way, life and truth--in Jesus Christ..

Amongst even those who claim to be Muslims, there is an attitude of open doors for change which has been shut out for a long time. This need is also ripe in the Republic of Somalia which the author visited. The Somali are a kind and torrent people, despite of the belief of otherwise. It is no wonder that there are Somali Christians because God in Christ Jesus has a witness among them.

Those seriously engaged in evangelism in Northern Kenya have reported great interest in Christian videos. Such missionaries are worthy of our respect, for the sacrifice required by evangelization of Northern Kenya is more than many can bear today.

The National Christian Council of Kenya, the Methodist Church in Kenya, the African Inland Church and Mission, the Presbyterian Church of East Africa, the Anglican Church of the and the Catholic Church all have been deeply involved in an effort to make Northern Kenya a ground for Church activities.

Such efforts have been rewarded, even in the most Muslim strongholds, by the ideal "Christian Community Churches" in Mandera, Wajir Garissa and Marsabit. This is one of the most important ventures that the churches in Kenya have ever been involved in.

The author recalls worshipping in all these churches where a real unity prevails, and the denominational bias is temporarily forgotten. Indeed, the church needs to learn from this, the mission that the modern nation and society needs.

People like the Redille, in general, seem less receptive to Islam or Christianity, they need something practical and meaningful. They are not alone because most people are tired or fed up with the traditional religiosity.

Religious fatalism seem to advocates idleness, endless reciting of prayers, and reducing humans to only a mechanism for reciting scriptural verses instead of a rational being who is in need of a good balance of spirituality and social awareness.

Observations and Reflections;

To speak from personal observation, the author made eight different routes to the Northern Kenya between 1970-1994.

1st Research Route;

The first route started from St. Paul's Theological College, Limuru, with Dieter Lorenz ,then a theological student of Hamburg University, took us to Isiolo, the doorway through Archer's Post, Wamba, Lodugokwa, Kisima to Maralal.

While there, attempts were made to visit Lake Turkana (Rudolf) through Poror and Baragoi, but we had to return, for the route to North Hor was impassible.

2nd Research Route;

The second route, after returning to Isiolo, started from there through Archer's Post, Seroleyi, Laisamis, Lukoloko to Marasabit where, after some stay, we went through Choma and Sololo to Moyale where we based ourselves and visited Ethiopia before leaving through Debel and Buna to Wajir.

3rd Research Route

The third route started from Wajir through Maddu Gashi to Garissa where a stay at the Boys Town gave us a good research opportunity.

4thResearch Route

The fourth route started from Garissa back to Wajir where we made our final research observations and left through Garba Tula to Isiolo. That concluded the first tour of the research in 1970.

2nd Research Tour;

On the second research tour, the author was accompanied by his wife ,a graduate of Kamwenja Teachers College and then a school teacher at Wamahiga Primary School,SabaSaba.

The Safari started from Muthithi Parish, Murang'a County, to Isiolo.

5th Research Route;

The **Fifth Route** started from there through Garba Tula, Wajir El Wak to Mandera, where the other made observatory research with good visits to Ethiopia and Somalia Republics.

6th Research Route;

The **Sixth Route** was the return from Mandera through El Wak to Wajir where we spent the night.

7th Research Route;

The **Seventh Route**, started from Wajir through Garba Tulla, Garissa, Mwingi, Kitui, Kithimani to Thika and finally back to the Parish Center, Muthithi.

In both experiences of different years, the author noted the advancement of Islam in the local communities. Also, one cannot help to note many hopelessness in people's attitudes, with no work to do. Some gather around tree shades and building posts, especially in small towns.

A new visitor, in some places, particularly if he looks European, is surrounded and attracted by being shown small beautiful stones, ornaments and some traditional weapons, etc. If the stranger chooses to purchase any of the items, he attracts even more people who bring their things too.

One of the future problems is that the people in Northern Kenya are awaking up to the new challenges and changes. Unless the Church does something specific now to present them with the Gospel that is based on "Love your neighbor as yourself"; they will awake only to find their roots dead, in extreme Islamic ideological soil, which could be no more than a violent and terrorizing sinking sand.

Without the reception of Islam as a culture and way of life, especially among the Islamized people and the underdevelopment, brought by colonialism and the lack of concern by the ensuing independent governments; Northern Kenya would have been easy to evangelize and develop.

Right now, the Islam mission is being geared and planned in this part of the nation. Therefore, it is high time the Christian church take seriously the fact that Jesus Christ died for all people; which makes the Christian Gospel unique in its concern for to all, in saving the human soul and its mission is to all the world cultures.

This is no time to sit down and assume that the whole of Northern Kenya is alright, it is still not yet evangelized, underdeveloped, under harsh ecological conditions, with hurting communities that must concern us all.

The concern is to "go ... and make disciples for Jesus Christ."

This is the church's responsibility, and it should awake to it.

Right now, as mentioned before, some churches are carrying considerable evangelistic endeavors--mainly the Protestants, the African Inland Church amongst the Turkana and others; the Presbyterian Church of East Africa amongst the Samburu; the Church of the Province of Kenya (Anglicans) Bible Church Missionary Society amongst the Borana and others; and the Methodist Church of Kenya amongst the Borana, Oromo and Somali. These and other Protestant groups do both the spiritual and social work amongst these people, giving the spiritual aspect the first priority.

The National Christian Council of Kenya and the Roman Catholic Missions, which are in almost every place in these areas, put more emphasis on the social and material sphere. It is no wonder one priest told the author that in Northern Kenya the cross is irrelevant and his operation is under a humanitarian flag instead.

Unfortunately, there are those who operate their enterprises without the consideration of the cross, but since most of them admit that evangelism is none of their concerns, this is understandable.

It is hard for the author, in the context of the Church mission, to separate the social and spiritual aspects of humanity as composed in the Evangel (or Gospel).

Evangelism is the balancer of the two concerns, the spiritual first and secondly, the social. Mission concern may begin with social emergency response but must then end up with the spiritual meaning and liberation.

Any person is an individual first before becoming a part of a society. He has a soul first before having the container, the body. There is no use in giving food and clothing to poor people if you do not show them how to eat the food without being selfish and how to put on their clothes without pride. .At the same time, teach the need of a Savior who can deliver or redeem their lives from sin and misery by providing constant life, the basis of existence.

The Human being to be free as a whole, needs salvation through Jesus Christ who really is the only true satisfaction for the human soul, mind and body.

To meet one need and leave the other is far from the Christian Gospel whether a person excuses himself on humanitarian grounds or not; he must recognize this.

The main danger and problem in Evangelism would be, or always is, when it is based on one side of human need. Northern Kenya will require a real holistic evangelism, requiring the spiritual and psycho-physical spheres of life be adequately addressed. Empty religious prayer recital, like the ones found amongst most of our societies in Kenya, rarely liberate the human soul..

Wajir and Mandera, being the Northern most, are Islamic strongholds representing the Somali are the leading in population there. The fact that these are Somali towns makes them appear Islamic by nature.

Most people, unfortunately, confuse Islam here with tradition. In other words, they would say "to be born a Somali is to be born a Muslim". This attitude has become a main thought in the Somali philosophy of life.

Considering this religious, philosophical and cultural confusion, it is very hard to find Somali Christians. Also, there are some that are unacceptable in their homesteads; most of the Somali Christians are amongst the educated, living outside of Northern Kenya.

Even for those who claim to be Muslim, most of them can hardly tell you the history of Islam or define what they mean in their belief. They are just victims of a religious sentimentalism with no knowledge of the gospel truth that makes people free.

They just observed what comes to them through traders and far-travelling pastoralists who have met with self-styled religious propagandists who, on the basis of Somali brotherhood, gave them some ready-made religious answers to their spiritual, cultural and social needs.

They, in turn, brought it to the following generations without even any knowledge of writing or reading. Those of old have Islamized the young ones by nature.

This may not be unique to the Muslim community but it is a hard socialization and psychological and human situation to understand, but this is Northern Kenya's current situation.

The Somali tradition, life and experience has become so mingled or mixed up that it is now hard to understand their indigenous religion or philosophy. Unless one settles on the conclusion that Sunni Islam has become the religion of the Somali.

It is in Islam that Somalis, as a people, have lost their identity with a strict and harsh moral code, especially towards women. Women are in no way considered worthy of making any decision on important issues, either concerning life or society. She seems by tradition, a second-class person both in social and religious affairs.

Prostitution in privacy, which is not condoned becomes a solution to most of the problems encountered by women either married or unmarried. Those married suffer, especially if a divorce occurs expectantly.

Divorce is common and permissive in Islamic societies, provided there is a witness to four times recital of the words "I divorce you ... I divorce you." I divorce you ... I divorce you." This is especially dangerous when a man tries to escape family responsibilities and settles done with another woman as a wife.

He can just as well get his friend as a witness, and that makes the divorce legal according to Islamic law. If such a woman is in a town or near one, she chooses private prostitution as opposed to open prostitution, still claiming to be religious just like any other.

In the case of an unmarried woman, prostitution does not come automatically as an escape of the traditional system of keeping girls in closets.

 This is justified by the excuse that they will become prostitutes if exposed to the eyes of boys by preventing them from going to school where they can learn more and become intellectually developed.

The girls comfort their minds by thinking and setting their hopes on marriage.

However, when marriage does not occur in time, they break the parental traditional, religious and moral wall and establish themselves in towns as prostitutes, private or public.

In places where prostitution is legal as most people claim, such as Ethiopia, which is Northern Kenya's neighboring state, it causes a social problem. This is especially true when those working in the Northern Kenya cross the border and fall victim to venereal diseases in their passion for sexual and immoral satisfaction with prostitutes.

For most people who come from southern parts of Kenya (up country as they call it), it is one of their moral and spiritual problems. Mind you, most of these people are married with their families left in their down country homes. Because of the false illusion that one cannot exist without sex, they go to the distant places by the wrong way for satisfaction.

Many people are dismissed by others as if, they reaped what they have sown in one way or the other. In some cases, most of these people become really sick because they are ashamed to go and heal their "wounds of sin" in their home country where they are known. In most cases, an Ethiopian private physician in engaged and after paying a considerable amount of money one gets the needed treatment.

It is very hard for a Christian to live in places of prostitution if his faith is not deeply rooted in Jesus Christ as the answer to life. He needs a deep conviction that man does not live on drinking, bread, and sex alone but by the word of life.

Kenyan history has recorded that there was a time the Somali, under the name the "Shifta"(which is Bandit in Ethiopian Amharic language) tried to secede from Kenya to join the northern-east neighboring Somali Republic.

61

However, under the "Arusha Agreement", after four years of war, President Mzee Jomo Kenyatta and the Somali President agreed to negotiations and eventually, a settlement was made in 1967, for an end to the bloody and bitter struggle.

The war, like any war, left thousands fatherless, motherless and homeless. After the war, almost every town was full of misery and hopelessness.

This writer still recalls a time when children ran from place to place, hungry and thirsty, begging for anything that would meet their needs. One could not help but have tears run down his cheeks to see these young ones often getting rubbish from waste pits just in search of food.

Most of the children were sick. Their eyes were going almost blind, yet with a can in their hands they still begged all over. Their limbs were as thin as sticks and their bellies were swollen from malnutrition. Indeed, for this author, this made him see more misery than he ever knew or thought existed in the world.

At the time of research, most of the children had been settled by the Catholic Church and other projects by Protestant Missions, especially around Lake Turkana (in the Boys Town in Garissa and the Girls Town in Wajir. Projects by the National Christian Council of Kenya and the Government have reduced the problem.

El-wak still remains an example of this problem where such children still roam in the hot and sweeping deserts in search for food and shelter either day or night. Continuing the observation, there are thousands of victims of starvation and full of disease and malnutrition.

The author's emotions could not be controlled, neither could he stop shedding tears, as he watched these people suffering from neglect, destitution and hunger, while there are others living in mansions elsewhere in the country, with no compassion at all.

To dream alone of such a condition disturbs the mind until one cannot sleep. Here was a bad human condition in reality.

Above Maralal, especially south of Lake Turkana in Baragoi, a visit to the hospital alone was enough for breaking a hardened heart to the misery in the environment. Young babies could be seen clinging on the side of their dying mothers.

It is a situation that makes you not understand why. A situation that makes your body ache, your legs heavy and your mouth open wide in dismay, grief, and concern.

All different ages of people suffer from these conditions. The aged, the adolescents, the strong Samburu or Redille Moran (youth-warriors), children, mothers and fathers all are victims of these social problems.

The soup-kitchens projects also provided food to the hungry. Some privileged people could easily exploit the distribution for selfish ends. The most moving thing in these places, especially in Marsabit, was that miserable conditions welcomed everybody who visited these projects.

In Wajir, the same thing prevailed, demanding the churches' evangelical action to provide food, shelter, clothing and, above all, love.

With hot weather, desert grounds and the wind blowing and sweeping sand dust all over men, women and children with hungry, thirsty, and sad faces could be seen in the Government Administration Centers, National Christian Council of Kenya, mission Centers, and soup kitchens in hope of a pound of ration. These are people who indeed know hunger in reality.

The danger of draught is altogether another threat. One pastoralist may boast a herd with more than a thousand cattle but within a short time the draught can reduce them to nil (as it happened in 1970), leaving people without any possible means of living. At the same time, many people suffered from diseases, in as much as it is easy to get sick when you are hungry.

One cannot really visit the Northern Kenya without being alarmed by the great need for help, especially food and other means of living. There is an extreme poverty among many of the nomadic pastoralists.

Hunger and thirst act as the reflection for this. For example, a single day in August 1971, more than 10,000 people visited the Soup-Kitchen and the feeding centers. Those who could not reach the centers struggled in silence and suffered until they met a slow death.

Both hunger and thirst are, in themselves, acute human problems requiring special attention because without food and water life becomes empty. It is just like a machine without energy.

Young children in Northern Kenya should not have to run around towns gathering crumbs or bones from unpleasant places. Old men and women do not have to die in the open desert because there is no pint of water, while in homes people in other parts have plenty of water to use and waste.

If Christians, really care about our Northern Kenya neighbors, they could help transform these sweeping deserts to the glory of God, where human beings become whole and enjoy life abundantly.

This is possible if we give our lives and energies to help these people in all ways possible, showing them of the love of God. It is only by doing this that the situation can be transformed.

History has shown us that a place where hunger and thirst exists can be transformed into a place of plenty of food and water. Therefore, in Northern Kenya there is still hope.

The challenge is to give both the spiritual and physical food. This is an application of the practical Gospel (Evangel) of the love of God to the world in Jesus Christ. It is Christianity in action bringing the compassion of the Savior in a revolution that transforms both the soul and spirit and body.

.

5 SOCIO-ECONOMIC DEVELOPMENT AND

POVERTY ERADICATION

THE SOCIO- ECONOMIC PROBLEMS

A.   Economic

1. **Extreme Poverty**

Extreme poverty is one of the most visible social and economic problems among the Northern Kenya Pastoralist. This is brought about partly by natural causes, such as lack of rain, which leads to a lack of grass for cattle. As a result, a great number of them die. Loss of cattle leaves a person with little, if anything, to cling to.

Being without cattle in any family or homestead automatically qualifies this as poverty because the chief means of economy, in such a pastoral country, is cattle.

Everybody in the pastoral life depend on cattle plus sheep, goats, donkeys and camels for food (milk and meat); clothing (the skin); and shelter (where skins or cow dung are used for building small huts in which to dwell).

It is, therefore, easy to guess what happens or would happen if a draught gets rid of a number of cattle herds. The draught that hit this place in 1970-71, is an example for even today by the roadside near water pools countless bones are scattered all over from animals that died.

It is a painful experience when one looks at such a situation. Life here is simple and ancient in form. When the chief means of livelihood is in trouble, people suffer in unpredictable ways.

The writer knows what such a depravity would mean because walking in the "manyattas", the living places where the homestead is based, he was in the midst of this struggle. There was nothing else to do but focus one's eyes on the sky where the sun burns to the world below with a high degree.

Here, poverty is not considered on what one neighbor has and what the other doesn't have. It is not a matter of comparison, but an extreme condition where the hopes of the future is cut from the present.

That is, tomorrow is not hopeful in any way since today, itself, is not promising. The only hope is death at anytime, anywhere, an anyhow. It is very hard for a person like this writer who comes from the middle class family (neither poor nor rich) to understand poverty as seen from the Northern Kenya context.

Having no shoes as a little boy is considered poverty in certain circles, but that is not it, for in such a situation one has to look at the immediate necessities, needs and satisfaction.

As a son of a mixed farmer (to use a personal experience), the writer's family depended on both stock and crops for their economy. If a draught hit and the cattle produced less milk, the already stored food from the land could be used for both human and animal consumption.

If both crop and stock were hit at the same time, what was saved from the advantage of both served our needs. That, indeed, is the advantage of those who are both agriculturalists and pastoralists.

The Northern Kenyans who are only pastoralists and this agricultural disadvantage makes it difficult in this semi-desert land for anything from grass, sources of water, animals and even people to survive in times of draught.

It is, altogether, a time of hopelessness with no refuge whatsoever except death. For some, it is a good time to sit down, as one struggles for survival, and keep assuring one's self "Ni Shauri Ya Mungu"--it is God's will. It is the depravity of the chief means of economy that is the main cause of poverty.

If the chief means of economy stops being the only means and is supplemented with another, probably things would change. Livestock alone cannot be the only means of living. Agriculture has been proven as a good supplement, and a good balance between the two is desirable.

It is hard to think of some parts of Northern Kenya in regard to agriculture because the vegetation is not desirable for crops.

However, there are some parts, especially in Turkana and Samburu Counties along the Great Rift Valley, where crops can and, in fact, grow. In other areas, only grass desirable to desert animals (small shrubs or trees) grow.

Yet, if the Israelis were able to transform the Sinai Desert into dwelling agricultural areas, the desert in Northern Kenya can be transformed.

Almost in all towns now people are finding that plants can grow. It is no wonder one can get a good maize in Mandera. Life would be especially unbearable here to strangers if there were no traders.

The traders have their corrupt sides also. Most of them oppress the poor. They do it by exploitation; say for example, someone is in need of flour (unga), the trader places the price very high so that he forces the poor nomad to give a cattle for only a few pounds of the item in question.

In most cases, they buy a number of cattle at very low prices. They then transport these cattle to other parts of the country and sell them at very high prices. These are those selfish people who take advantage of the situation for their own ends.

There is no wonder as to why they would like the situation to stay as it is. Because they possess the only means of transportation, there is no other alternative. The poor become poorer while the rich become richer; the ignorant is made more ignorant while the wise become wiser.

As mentioned elsewhere, famine and thirst are yet the other social and economic problems. A good example of these problems can be derived from a recent 1970-71 draught which really caused an alarm about the condition in the Northern Kenya area.

The local newspapers appealed for food, water, clothes and shelter.

People everywhere saw their own conditions as the draught became

worse, from Turkana to the Mandera Districts and down to Isiolo.

The condition was unbearable; people died as animals fell dead.

The draught not only killed thousands of cattle but it also left a great

famine and thirst as the grass and water places dried up.

6 PEACE ,SECURITY,FOOD SUPPLY AND

WATER SOURCES

2.Famine and Thirst

There still exists a hunger and thirst that is unbearable in this part of the country, which threatens peace and security of the people.

Here, herdsmen battle daily against it as the thermometer often rises above 120 degrees in the shade. You can, therefore, imagine the difference.

The nomadic Pastoralists take no notice of legal boundaries when they search for water and grass and often wander in homeland Kenya and Ethiopia. They often turn to marauding--hence comes the name "Shifta" (for Somali Nomads) and Ethiopia word for burgand. This fact was one of the causes of the "Shifta" guerilla war against the Kenya rule for more than four years.

Altogether the problem of transportation affects the Northern Kenya in many ways. For one thing, most of the people don't raise any food, and if they raised any, it would be limited to one kind, such as meat and milk.

Therefore, it is appropriate that they have to get some food from local traders. In order for the traders to obtain the food, they have to transport it from a down-country town to their respective shops.

In most cases, the honest traders operate at a loss, while the dishonest ones get richer at the expense of the people they might consider psychologically inferior.

This is very bad because each individual has both the negative and positive elements in himself. No one needs to dominate the other on grounds of privileges.

The Government ought to devote considerably more attention to the problem of transportation. It's important to the whole nation and not only for the local small communities.

In this respect, the Government should ensure good transportation. Not only should the Government promote transportation, it should also regulate it in all the extreme northerly places.

In places where the present small roads run through mountains and large rivers, a lot of oil is consumed as the vehicles reduce their speed. These roads should be cut down to avoid operation by the Government and individual companies to go at a loss.

By improvement of transportation, the present picture of Northern Kenya might change.

From experience, the writer can remember places where one had to wait for several weeks to get transportation to another place. In most cases you do not get any.

In almost all cases, you find women with young babies, old ladies with their backs bent from years of starvation waiting for weeks to go somewhere, either to a hospital or elsewhere.

At the same time the sun keeps burning up the grounds and the sweeping wind, typical to desert places, sweeps and blows sandy dust upward towards the sky in a constant motion, releasing the dust on helpless human bodies and eyes.

The problem of transportation, which can reduce hunger and thirst if solved, has in its nature another subordinator which is also a real problem, that of communication.   Both transportation and communication go together.   To solve one would mean a solution to the other in one way or the other.

.

7 TECHNICAL POLITICS:COMMUNICATIONS
AND TRANSPORTATION

B.Political

1.Communication

The development of any country depends on two most important factors, transportation and communication.

Transportation would not be possible without communication. Each depends on the other, and both are closely linked in a way that it is difficult to separate them.

Without these two factors, our whole way of life would crumble. There could be no government, no nations, no schools, no trade and almost no entertainment. Our modern and model society would not exist without these.

However, in Northern Kenya this is one of the obstacles that keeps it underdeveloped. As far as communication is concerned, there are no adequate post office facilities, apart from a few in the main district Centers. Most of these have no telephones.

Those who deal with medical or other emergencies use radio calls. Apart from letters, there is no other means to reach one's friends or relatives in the northerly districts or down country.

In most places, language is another communication barrier to sharing information. Often, there is little said in the mass media about these people apart from `tribal' crashes.

Newspapers and magazines are hardly found in these places, and if one succeeds in getting one in the District Center, it is a few days old. Some happen to have come with those who travelled to the down country.

Radios, on the other hand, are the only effective means of bringing information to the people of Northern Kenya. Unfortunately, Radio Mogadishu (Republic of Somalia) seems to be more powerful here, thereby, earning a certain amount of popularity.

Communication, as a basic human activity here, is far from being adequate and, in most cases, available. Since the government should give special attention to this problem, the writer had found it appropriate to consider it under political problems.

The citizens of the Republic of Kenya, by all means, should get better information about the current affairs in the nation as a whole. They also need the latest news and education about livestock prices and crops; the later may not be considered important.

The few schools there are should have good books and teachers to help in sharing information regarding the world we live in. Ki-Swahili should be used as the language of instruction to overcome some of the language barriers that already exist, hindering the free sharing of information and overcoming of cultural barriers.

Travelling on the roads, especially in the day time, is very risky to vehicles because of possibilities of tire punctures. The writer recalls during his travel in government and civilian vehicles that none of these were without punctures on their journeys.

This was partly because of extreme heat but, basically, because of the bad roads.

Most of the roads have very sharp stones which break down vehicles easily. Maralal-Baragoi is especially one of the worst. As the hills reduce the speed of the vehicles, the fuel consumption is increased, resulting in a great loss to the operator of such a personal or public transportation.

2.Transportation

Good roads are in great demand because of the distance between town centers. Up until today, there are only a few, and these few are not of any good standard

An all-weather road such as the new Nairobi-Addis Ababa road is of a preferable standard. All-weather roads like the one from Isiolo to Moyale, across the Ethiopia border, are the kind that answers the need of Northern Kenya.

With different kinds of people travelling on such roads, a new opportunity would open for the tribes in Northern Kenya, presenting to them an opportunity to go beyond and outside their environments. It is justifiable to assume that if roads are better, more bus service than the Northern and Eastern Bus Service, the Quick Bus Service, "Kangelikya", and the East African Bus Service (all of which are limited in operation) would be on the move and more people would be travelling.

The bus companies that have tried to operate in Northern Kenya experienced a great loss in terms of mechanical breakdowns. Most of them had to stop operations completely.

During the time of this research, the writer had to use individual vehicles which, in some cases, charged him great amounts mercilessly and under un-preferable conditions. In cases of necessity, this was, however, better than spending weeks waiting for means of transportation that might never come.

One of the things that would be of great help to Northern Kenya is to be exposed to agricultural information. At the same time, telephones, as a means of communication, should be available for public use despite the problems there are in establishing postal facilities.

There should be a program geared at meeting this need. Establishment of better communication facilities would help the people of Northern Kenya share the fruits of independence and development with others all over the nation.

Enough information should be available to other people about Northern Kenyans so that they may understand and seek means of helping them not only in times of hunger and thirst but always.

The people of Northern Kenya do not have to live in ignorance. They are worthy of enjoying the benefits of the nation just as any other citizen in our democratic republic where every human being should be considered important.

After all, recent anthropology tells us the ancient remains of the oldest man were found around Lake Turkana, a part of Northern Kenya.

To create a patriotic and spirit minded Somali and Borana, there should be a better communication program among the two countries. Considering the geographical set up in the country, Nairobi, the capital of the Government, national operations, and other affairs is quite a distance to the extreme northerly districts.

Without adequate communication, there can be no interest in the local and national affairs among the nomadic groups.

Unfortunately, the communication system is not adequate, apart from the local administration offices which partly help the people understand our nation, its society, government, law (courts) and towns.

This author existed in Northern Kenya as a lonely individual with the feeling of being a stranger. There was no difference between a visit to Southern Ethiopia or North-western Somalia where one had to behave, feel and think like an alien. One, in most cases is cut off from the regular people who behave in a way acceptable to one' mode of existence.

In Northern Kenya people behave in a completely different way and live in a different social surrounding. One of the wonders of nature was the big vultures (birds) with their black and white suits.

These, in almost all circumstances in Wajir, were the writer's closest companions as he walked in the hot desert sand to different places. It was also wonderful to watch camels coming in and going out in these centers.

The whole communication structure was different. One, especially in times of doing research questioning, had to use a lot of different psychological approaches to start a conversation with a local person. While some were friendly others seemed so hostile that one was dismissed to ask any questions lest he offended such a person. Others forced us to talk and in such a challenge one had, by all means, to express himself in a way that he is well understood.

In this respect, it is recommended for any person with a desire to reach and help these people. O should first have an idea, if not a good knowledge, of their cultural background, including language if possible. This would give such a person a real powerful weapon to overcome the old communication problem on a personal level.

In order to overcome or deal with the communication problem, we must consider too the problem of transportation. As we mentioned elsewhere, both communication and transportation are companions, born together as twins by development and civilization. In the extreme Northerly Frontier Districts of Kenya both remain yet a problem to be solved.

The problem is an alarming one; there is no doubt about that. Roads are few and bad, and there is no public means of transportation. The main roads only lead to the main divisional and county centers. Most of these are not suitable or motor- able in rainy seasons. The only solution would then be air transportation which is by no means adequate.

For the sick patients living in isolated places, there are no means of getting medical attention unless one struggles in the bushy desert to come to a hospital. Only a few make it, if any.

Some choose a medicine man (traditional doctors) who in almost all cases makes the person even sicker; at the same time, the medicine man is paid a great amount of goats from the main Manyattas to the other.

This could solve the problem of medical care and also for law enforcement forces like the police who could rush to a crime scene within moments of being notified. A limit to the shifting would easily develop, thereby making people feel a sense of settlement.

8 PASTORAL PROBLEMS AND

NOMADIC SUBSISTENCE

A. The Problem

1. Comparison

The comparison of both the cultural and social-ecological problems are similar.

The section on social problems dealt with people as a society and things concerning their economy and ecology, extreme poverty, famine and thirst. Mostly, these are problems that seem to be purely dealing with and touching n the Government or State and its political structures such as communication and transportation.

The cultural section dealt with those problems dealing with or related to the people's values, such as cattle, their way of life and their nomadic work. At the same time, it looked at their definition of religion, both traditional and Islam (most of those already Islamized). On the other hand, the ethical and moral practices were observed, especially in relationship to their families, friends and strangers. Some groups were elaborated more than others, at the same time avoiding the claim to be an authority and being unfair in the observation.

This is partly because some of their family action,s patterns and existing values constituted a particular problem. At the same time, the writer felt the necessity of more analysis on a particular social structure.

Therefore, the problems mentioned here as cultural could be, at the same time, defined as social. Both are inseparable because there is no society without a culture nor is there a culture apart from a society.

However, to deal with the problems in Northern Kenya, one feels that some of these, if not all, come directly from what people do rather than what they are.

Some problems are defined as cultural while those which come as a result of what people are in relation between person or groups are classified as social.

In comparison they are all the same in one way or the other as far as they deal with persons and the problems that face them in a particular culture, age and situation.

Analyzing such problems as lack of food, water, and shelter leads us to an examination of the particular people's culture, their occupation, clothes, skills, political and traditional organization.

To be more appropriate, the Northern Kenya problems are socio-cultural in nature, affecting the lives of these thousands of people in this vast desert environment and society in their different ways of carrying their activities.

9 THE QUESTION OF EVANGELISM AND

DEVELOPMENT

2.   The Results

This results in one of the most acute problems as far as the mission of the Church of concerned--the problem of "being not yet evangelized".

In other words, the socio-cultural problems in Northern Kenya have affected its being evangelized and this has affected the Church's sole mission to the world.

We should realize, as a matter of reality and experience based on existential facts, that the basic need of every human being is a spiritual one. Basically, the problem of human beings, as a society, has to do with the wholeness of persons.

To look at problems from one side alone is to be ignorant of the wholeness and unity of man who is a spiritual and social being. Altogether, it is always important to realize that all man's social, cultural or political problems are a reflection of the spiritual condition within and the needs outside.

Human beings, as a rational beings according to the Scripture (Bible) are created in the image of his Creator who is the Almighty, the Living God, the giver, supplier and distributor of life. In Him there is the element that can truly make man human.

This element is based on love and care that no one should suffer. What makes man alive is the fact that the soul of man is constantly God conscious. Thus, humans becomes a spiritual creature with a deep yearning for God's salvation, care, love and peace.

This is why in Northern Kenya, even those tribes who do not accept Islamization still look up yonder to the mountains in a deep yearning to God as the final answer to their religious need. They have, in fact, their own beliefs and patterns of worshipping.

Also, there is a possibility of worshipping the wrong beings, gods or deities. We cannot, in any respect, forget that this reminds us that there is a great need for God in the life of every human being-- civilized or primitive, depending on your definition. It is for this reason that the socio-cultural problems become problems to evangelization in the Church's approach to them.

Evangelism is the spiritual dealing with human beings not minimizing or adding anything foreign to their being and nature. Both social and spiritual aspects are necessary to each other as negative is necessary to the positive.

Any other sort of evangelism dealing with anything different from the wholeness of man is contrary to the Christian gospel (or evangel) and the person of the Evangel-Jesus Christ who deals with the whole person.

In dealing with the complete man, Jesus Christ spiritually liberates man by reconciling him with God, the loving Father from whom he has been separated and alienated by his own sin and disobedience.

For more than half a century, the Northern Kenya has been closed to Evangelization, Missionization or presentation of the good news. Now that the doors are open, there is little evangelism being done. The basic obstacle to evangelization is nothing more than the mentioned socio-cultural problems dealt herewith in a more or less general and observance way.

What is being called for now is action in Christ to deal with them and solve them in a forward pressing mission.

10 CONCLUSION:DESERT GOSPEL

B. The Solution

1.Development

Having presented the problem which comes as a result of socio-cultural problems, the next step is to suggest a two-fold solution which presents a way to the answer.

First, there should be a program geared to developing Northern Kenya. In other words, the development is the first stage to the solution of the social-cultural problems.

The Government, which right now is involved in many development projects (Harambee), should be considering the rural as well as the semi-urban administration centers.

Northern Kenya can be agriculturally productive if better programs are geared towards such. The government has to allocate some funds for the area, after which a settlement of the nomads would follow. Most of the people in this part of the country have a deep interest in a change like agriculture.

Education should also be included in the development program or plan because by creating more schools most of the children will get their education and learn better ways of understanding their environment.

The sort of education needed in Northern Kenya is mass education, involving even the adults, the semi-education and the illiterate. These people, in their scattered manyattas, should also be taught more about livestock.

This can be done if, for example, each person is given some 50 to 100 acres of land for ranching and farming and are then helped to learn the fact that the quality might be better than quantity as far as cattle is concerned.

Teaching these people to help themselves is the only great secret of development in a place like this where people are not used to such work as digging or any other skills. Such teaching would have to be shown in practice or action rather than in theory.

Talking to them in meetings (barazas) and refusing them food in times of need is no way of teaching anything. They should be given food that has been donated by faithful and sympathetic people for famine relief.

This place should, by all means, be made to become of age and keep pace by improvement of the existing development. Experts should check the regional soil and climate.

If agriculture becomes possible, then utilize irrigation and modern farming techniques. An example of this can be seen in different places where seasonal crops and other crops grow. Tomatoes, onions, peppers, bananas, advocates, lemons, grapes, limes tangerines, papaya, cantaloupes, water melons and even rice are but a few of the crops that are being grown in experimental places is some northerly counties.

Development, indeed, is one of the means to solve the problems; however, development alone is not an adequate step to the solution. Development is the method the Government is using to approach these socio-cultural problems. This alone is not adequate in consideration from a Church's mission point of view.

2..<u>Evangelism</u>

The second approach, which fulfills the spiritual solution to these problems, is Evangelism which is beyond development.

The scriptural definition of evangelism is proclamation of God's Gospel of love, which indeed is the development of the whole man, so that as he is liberated and set free from poverty, oppression and hunger he might enjoy life more abundantly.

Evangelism, being affected by the socio-cultural problems in this part of the country, is a part of the problem and, therefore, a part of the solution--if not the solution.

In other words, if this region is to be developed into a more lively place in which human beings can exist, the Church must take Evangelism has been taken seriously the local situation is radically changed. This is the greatest need among the Northern Kenya communities.

They need the loving God who offered His Son as Saviour to a world of hostility, poverty and other problems. Evangelism is the answer to the socio-cultural problems because these concern a humanity in need of peace, love and hope.

The Church should, therefore, be ready to present the person of the evangel to the masses in the Northern Kenya who die in poverty, hunger and thirst.

Thanks to God there are churches in Northern Kenya who take this challenge seriously, healing those stricken by disease and feeding hungry stomachs and at the same time giving the message of salvation, peace and hope to hungry and empty hearts.

The Church's approach to Northern Kenya's problems may worsen the situation. If evangelism is abandoned, the whole mission of the Church will be a failure.

Through observations and interviews with different people it was revealed that the spiritual need demands the first priority in order to transcend the social, political, cultural and economic problems.

It is useless to feed and clothe a man with an empty heart for he may as well commit suicide and bring your efforts to a nil. Any human being with an empty heart is truly unbalanced and is in need of a balance in life.

This is where evangelism becomes relevant. To "go to preach, teach, instruct and build", is the solution. may the Church plan evangelistic programs for development of Northern Kenya as soon as possible.

Possibly, by the year 2050 the whole land might appear another North Africa which, after the failure of the Church to stand strong, was swept by the Islamic forces, making it hard not only for the existence of the Church but even for evangelization.

With the existence of Interdenominational Christian Community Churches, which the writer visited in several towns, mission and evangelization is possible now or never. What is needed is a united mission effort.

The time has come for the African Church to evangelize her own unreached people, of course, avoiding the mistakes that historically have characterized the many denominations in our land, and even sects that have created a spirit of disunity and enmity.

Prologue:

Now the challenge is before the Churches, for predominantly desert areas of Northern Kenya is NOT YET EVANGELIZED. The Gospel (INJILI), must be delivered NOW for the NEED for development of people is great..

Epilogue: Sources and Comments

1.Personal observation and interpretation.

2.Used socio-scientific methodology in research.

3.Interviewed Government Officials, and the local leaders and people.

4.Consultation with friends involved in service, teaching or business in these areas.

5.Only a little, if any, written materials exists on the subject.

6.As we enter the 21st century, more material seems to be forthcoming about the area. Personally this is only a beginning; more reflection, observation and research is needed as the area gets into the motion of change, development and evangelization.

ABOUT THE AUTHOR

The Revd. Prof. Dr. Nehemy Ndirangu Kihara was born in Nanyuki in Laikipia County of Kenya, East Africa.

He was educated at Timau in Meru County and Nairobi before graduating with a Licentiate of Theological Education from St. Paul's University (United Theological College), Limuru in Kiambu County.

He attained a Doctor of Philosophy (Ph.D.) in Anthropology, Sociology of Religion and Political Science from Emory University.

He graduated with honors and attained a Master of Divinity (M.Div.) in Social Ethics, Psychology of Religion and Counseling, from the Interdenominational Theological Center at the Clark Atlanta University Complex. He holds a Bachelor of Theology (B.Th.) in Biblical Literature and Geographic History from Christian International College.

As an Investigative Journalist and Radio Broadcaster this Independent Publisher hosted a weekend English and still hosts a weekly Swahili Community Show for Sagal Radio Services at WATB 1420 AM Station in Decatur, GA.

As an Interdisplinary Educator he taught Security Management and Police Studies for the Institute of Peace and Security Studies, (now known as the Department of Security and Correctional Science) of Kenyatta University in Nanyuki Campus, where he was the Coordinator of Humanities and Examinations Officer.

The Author also taught Introductory Psychology, Sociology, Criminal Procedure and Law of Evidence, Intelligence-Led Policing, Public Administration and General Management Principles among other units at the Nyeri and Embu Campuses.

He was an Adjunct Professor of Sociology/ Social Sciences at the

Atlanta Campus of Saint Leo University, Tampa, Fl. Taught such courses as Anthropology, Sociology, and Criminal Justice units as Social Theory, Drugs and Society, Marriage and Family, Research Methods, Human Behavior, among others He was an Adjunct Professor of Ethics at the Georgia Campus (Henry Medical Center) of the College of Health, University of St. Francis, Joliet, Ill.,

The Author was also the founding Moderating Bishop of the Ujamaa Nomadic Church -Without Borders, as a new church- mission initiative in US. He had also been an Urban Renewal/ Organizing Pastor of Beth Salem United Presbyterian Church, Columbus, Georgia. He served as an International Missionary in California, Iowa and New York, under the Mission to US program of the Presbyterian Church, USA.

As a Senior Lecturer at Kenyatta University, the Author taught African Culture, Belief Systems, Social Theory and Research Methods units in the Department of Philosophy and Religious Studies and also in the Department of Sociology. He was also an Activist Educator, who fought for academic freedom and excellence, which led to his unfair dismissal by the government which controlled the public universities and educational institutions.

Reverend Professor Ndirangu Kihara started his career a high school teacher and principal at Muthithi Secondary School, and then an ordained Church Minister of Muthithi Parish and the Stated Clerk of the wider Murang'a Presbytery of the Presbyterian Church of East Africa.